PRAISE FOR *KADDISH: BEFORE THE HOLOCAUST AND AFTER*

"In *Kaddish: Before the Holocaust and After*, Jane Yolen expertly weaves together figures of the Jewish faith like Goliath, Sarah, and Esther, alongside story characters such as Rumpelstiltskin, Anansi and Raven, all interconnected with known and unknown victims of the Holocaust. Calling upon a variety of poetic forms, Yolen takes the reader on a questioning journey through Jewish history, universal notions of motherhood, and the stark lens of the photograph, showing us 'This, the story / no one wants to tell, / must be told.' Full of anguish and insight, her poetry reveals that '… story sticks / when memory fails,' a powerful witness to both inhumanity and hope."

"In her poem, 'Shoes: Holocaust Museum, Washington D.C.,' Jane Yolen writes: 'I walk with foreknowledge into the museum, /sure it has nothing to teach me.' After all, hasn't she already written two of the classic Holocaust novels of our time, as well as numerous poems and yes, picture books on the subject? This is how I felt opening *Kaddish: Before the Holocaust and After*, Yolen's latest collection of poems. I've already read most of the 400 plus (no typo) books she has written; including all of her poetry for adults. And I've taught and lectured about Poetry of the Holocaust. What could possibly be left to learn? 'So why now,' the second stanza of 'Shoes,' continues, 'am I stunned, undone, incapable of moving on?' And that is how I felt as I closed the volume, 'stunned and undone' and, as Yolen says in another poem: 'uplifted, gifted, strengthened, /given breadth and breath.'"

—RICH MICHELSON, owner of R. Michelson Galleries in Northampton, Mass, is former poet laureate of Northampton

HOLY COW! PRESS BOOKS BY JANE YOLEN

Kaddish: Before the Holocaust
and After (2021)

The Bloody Tide:
Poems About Politics and Power (2014)

Ekaterinoslav: One Family's Passage to America,
A Memoir in Verse (2012)

Things to Say to a Dead Man:
Poems at the End of a Marriage and After
(2011)

KADDISH

BEFORE THE HOLOCAUST AND AFTER

BY JANE YOLEN

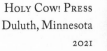

HOLY COW! PRESS
Duluth, Minnesota
2021

Author photograph by Jason Stemple.
Cover photo: The Berlin Memorial to the Murdered Jews of Europe, photo by D.Wang/Unsplash.
Book and cover design by Anton Khodakovsky.

Printed and bound in the United States.

First printing, Fall, 2021.

Library of Congress Cataloging-in-Publication Data

Yolen, Jane, author.
Kaddish: before the Holocaust and after / poems by Jane Yolen.
Description: Duluth, Minnesota : Holy Cow! Press, 2021.
Identifiers: LCCN 2021003222 | ISBN 9780998601090 (paperback)
Subjects: LCSH: Holocaust, Jewish (1939-1945)—Poetry. | LCGFT: Poetry.
Classification: LCC PS3575.O43 K33 2021 | DDC 811/.54—dc23
LC record available at https://lccn.loc.gov/2021003222

ISBN 978-0998601090

10 9 8 7 6 5 4 3 2 1

Holy Cow! Press projects are funded in part by grant awards from the Ben and Jeanne Overman Charitable Trust, the Elmer L. and Eleanor J. Andersen Foundation, the Lenfestey Family Foundation, Schwegman Lundberg & Woessner, P.A., the Ingber Family Philanthropic Fund of the Jewish Community Foundation of the Minneapolis Jewish Federation, and by gifts from generous individual donors. We are grateful to Springboard for the Arts for their support as our fiscal sponsor.

Holy Cow! Press books are distributed to the trade by Consortium Book Sales & Distribution, c/o Ingram Publisher Services, Inc., 210 American Drive, Jackson, TN 38301.

For inquiries, please write to: *Holy Cow! Press*, Post Office Box 3170, Mount Royal Station, Duluth, MN 55803.
Visit *www.holycowpress.org*

DEDICATION

For David Stemple, my late husband, of blessed memory, and my mother Isabelle Berlin Yolen who did not stay in this world long enough. They live in me.

CONTENTS

MITZVAHS AND MIRACLES

BEFORE

(WOMAN'S MIDRASHIM)

G-D'S CARTON

Egg cradle, the shell
held in an angel's arms,
a singularity waiting
to become a world.
No Big Bang here,
but the gentle opening
onto the fry pan
of the universe.
The only question—
will it be a watery Earth,
dry Mars, or your basic
everyday galactic scramble.

LIGHT

A word but not a word,
sound, but not sound,
a puff of air, hiss of breath,
shift of molecules
before there are molecules.

A star born before it has a name.
Garden planted with nouns.
Green not yet a color and yet
surely a color, pushing up
through what will one day be called
Ground Zero.

Something is born, from the earth,
from the star, vaguely man like,
woman like, but a surer touch
this time. Alike and not alike.

Something flies above their heads.
"Bird," the man figure says.
"Hawk," the woman figure says.
An argument from the beginning.

And all this with a single word.

FIRST WOMAN: LILITH

First woman,
agita,
as she stepped onto
the world's
earliest stage,
would not lie
or lie under,
but lay about
recreating
herself.
For her sin
a womb
cursed,
with bursting
imps;
demon named,
shamed,
convicted,
evicted

from the garden
before Eve
ever got there.
Ever after
laughed
as her daughters
slithered
through
the startled grass,
passing out
apples
and placards,
all the while
agitating
for the vote,
and a seat
in Heaven
at God's right
hand.

EVE'S NAVEL

If it's true, as centuries teach,
that Eve's belly was as blank
of navel as a child's slate
before a single word
has been written across it,
then medical science is overthrown.
Her children born without sac,
floating about within
uncradled, unfed,
banging against ribs,
for she had all of hers,
bouncing off liver, lungs,
coils as wound as pilpul.
No wonder her boys came out
cranky and cross enough
to think of murder.

WHAT ABOUT GOLIATH

Yes, Goliath was a bully,
perhaps because of his size,
growth plates still open.

Yes, he was a name-caller,
mouth as wide as a platter,
spouting venom, shouting lies.

Yes, he rattled a stick
big enough to split a skull,
or trip someone running away.

Perhaps his father was mean,
or he'd been whipped
with a studded belt.

Perhaps he just wanted attention.
Or love. Or even like.
Perhaps he just wanted to be left alone.

But when he fell,
shattering the concrete,
everyone applauded.

Little David was lifted up,
held his slingshot out as evidence.
Violence was crowned.

Maybe there's a better way
than slingshots, hot shots, mugshots.
Better than becoming Goliath
ourselves.

SARAI/SARAH

Sister, cousin, wife,
how nice of him to
give you different names
for the uses of your body;
to turn from you in time of danger;
to hold from you the sacrifice
of your only son.

You are the future's cartoon,
its palimpsest, blueprint
of a woman's life.
Better you died on that road
than see what was wrought
in your name, your names,
Sarah, Sarai, mother of nations.

HAGAR IN THE WILDERNESS

Compared to the wilderness of the house,
the old woman screaming at my baby,
the one she wanted and did not want.
The old man making those side glances
when he thought she wasn't looking.
And me on my knees cleaning the carpet
where once again the child had spit up dinner.

Compared to the wilderness of the garden
where the old woman pulled up my flowers
with the ruthlessness of a king, kept the fig tree
for herself, planted useless flowers between the rows.
Where the greens were parceled out three-quarters
to them and none of the goat's milk was kept
for the baby and me.

Compared to that, the wilderness they sent me to
was Eden, and the serpent's patient voice
with the baby, and his name it spoke in sibilants,
the way she let him play with her coils,
made living there a home, the first real one
I was to have, and the last.

JUDGES 4:21

There is a wind blowing from the East.
The Caucuses has much to answer for.
There is no such thing as safety:
nets can always be withdrawn,
redistributed, tangled, set on fire, cut.

Move your tent, the enemy follows,
with his persuasive multitude of lies.
Don't open the flap, my head says,
but the heart, in its infinite kompromat,
lets the known invader in.

He looks at my breasts, reaches for my sex,
holds me in arms that stink with compromise.
He begs me to resist, dares me do it,
laughs at the gravity of my body,
sells me to the next highest bidder.

This is not how it should be,
our names, our numbers, our addresses
flung into the Cossack mud.
Raise the tent peg, sister, raise it high.
It is the way, the only way.

GIVEN LEAVE

The Jews leave
Levant,
all unleavened,

Left foot, right,
they cross
the Sea,

Bread sent down
from God's
own heaven.

A virtual
Pyrrhic
victory.

Old Pharaoh's
son's death
left behind.

When given leave,
don't leave
behind

Leaving
Egypt
on each mind.

A gift of hate
for some
mankind.

AN INTERVIEW WITH J

So, I met her where she sat
under a date tree, composing a psalm
about the fruit, its warmth in the mouth,
the invite of its Fall.
Not her usual which was praise for Judea.
Or rhapsodies on G-d, she calls Jahweh.
She writes one a day,
sends them out to subscribers.
It's how she makes her living.
She rarely gives interviews,
Some say she is too shy,
or as a woman, cannot be seen
talking to a man not her husband.
Actually, she has no husband.
"Who wants a woman," she tells me,
"who is always writing psalms,
instead of getting water from the well,
or putting a baby to her breast?"
I nod, woman to woman.
"I do what I do best," she adds,
"even if I do not sign my name
to the psalms as David did.
He was a king after all.
Signing his name to stuff—
even stuff he didn't do—
comes with the kingdom."
She said it was enough, *dayenu*,
to have Jahweh know she had written it.

"The greatest critic of all approves.
Some of it," she says, "is pretty hot stuff.
Though I made all of that up."
She's a spinster, which hereabouts
means an old virgin.
One passion—poetry.
"Dayenu?" I ask, smiling.
She nods and smiles back,
takes out another piece of parchment,
the interview clearly over.

HIDDEN FIGURES

Who knew, who would tell
on Esther hiding
in the king's own harem?

Or Ruth sent to lie down
at a landowner's feet?
Not Naomi, not Boaz.

Or Moses in plain sight,
drawn from water,
drawn from the Jews.

The old book is full
of such hidden figures,
made in the mirror

of their G-d,
who Himself hides in Nature,
in plagues, in whirlwinds.

Showing up when He wants.
or when He thinks He is needed,
but often far too late for thanks.

RUSULKA

She rises from the water, arms raised,
drops flooding her long, red hair
that so recently was as fluid as the river.

She looks at the shore's stoic banks
still covered with withered stalks,
birch weeping openly into the weir.

She stares at the farmland beyond,
where nothing grew last season,
or the season before, the farm's family fled.

She has been too long beneath the rills,
uncalled, unremembered, forgetting
her old promises of the much-needed rain.

She pulls herself into a weeping tree.
Unseen Cossacks cast their fish-hooked net,
drag her out, fling her into the furrows.

They call her Jew, spread her legs,
leave her on the ground, far from the river.
She dries from the inside out, too quick for tears.

The farm languishes, the river disappears.
So we treat our guardians, our stories,
our land, our world.

THE LAMED-VOV

I could not have raised such a son, to carry all that suffering,
till the heart, the mind is broken on that particular cross.
Like Sarah, hearing of the binding of Isaac, I would make a fist,
hold it to Heaven, give myself to the fire in his place.

Women need no last-minute ram from the Great Herdsman,
sent down a shaft of light, on tentative hooves.
Why make a cosmic joke of sacrifice?
We women understand this bloody job with every month.

Thirty-six Just Men? How kind of them to take on the mishigas,
when the world needs cleaning, ironing, diaper changes,
the ordinary stuff that befouls the human mind long before
swords, guns, bombs, admit their bleaker view.

THAT OLD ANTI-SEMITE JAKOB GRIMM

Rumpelstiltskin is a Jew.
I'm surprised you never noticed,
so bent over your critique of Breitbart,
children's stories lie unexamined.

Rump lives outside the city walls,
his only job turning straw into gold,
that old moneychanger. His nose resembles
a pick-axe. And who can pronounce his name?

Of course, he ate the queen's child;
at Easter, I would guess. The blood
will make his matzo. Should be hanged
or torn to pieces.

The oven is ready. Give him a chance,
and he'll walk right in.

G-D AS TRICKSTER

I am not looking at you, Anansi,
spinning your world wide web
in the place where humanity began.
Nor you Raven, a needle in water.
Or rabbit with your zigzag path
between the green truths.

I am looking squarely at you,
old Jehovah, pulling out the rug
from under our bare feet,
offering life, delivering death,
a garden full of prohibitions
without a real contract
spelling out the disaster
we will make of this world.

If Chance is the real ruler here,
Birth order definitive,
Storm the obligation,
why bother giving us brains?
Just throw the meat on the fire,
and let the sizzle begin.

THE SHOAH'S
MANY VOICES

THE CHILD, THE BEARS, THE WAR: 4 VIEWS

1. JEWISH CHILD WITH TEDDY BEAR, POLAND 1935

The caption is the story.
We already know everything about this child.
But Teddy Bear's religion is not noted.
Perhaps in this country bears go to church
not synagogue, drink holy wine
with a cracker on the tongue.
Perhaps he will not be shot upon arrival
or sent into an oven, where his dark hair burns
with a peculiar smell, his eyes become pools.
Perhaps TB's will be given a brown shirt,
black boots, a black gun.
He will join groups
of other church-going bears
marching in perfect cadence.
The child, already noted,
and delivered to eternity,
with Little Bear in his arms
is a mere checkmark on a ledger,
without a name, only a number,
disappearing out of his story
into history.
Was he Franz, David, Mordicai, Joel?
TB no longer remembers him,
the playroom, the window, the phone,
the chair where they sang silly songs,
laughed at jokes no one else found funny.
TB's oven only bakes bread
and little cakes cut with crosses.
They are sweet and delicious, like lies.
He eats them up, and sleeps
as a human child sleeps.

2. THAT BOY

That boy is a Jew, but who would know
without the caption? Perhaps he is really
German, Russian, Polish, Irish.
Maybe he is Scottish, Italian, Greek.
He plays with two bears,
one big, one little, missing
only Mama Bear who might
have been the one to warn them,
the one to carry the child
on her broad shoulders
out of danger.

That phone, its dial. I remember
the ring tones, always comforting.
Papa calling about coming home,
or Mrs. Sheffield, across the hall,
wanting a play date with her daughter.
Or the butcher to tell Mama
her order was ready.
Not the Commandant instructing you
to line up, take off your clothes,
march into the shower room,
where it only, ever, rains death.

3. I KNOW THIS CHILD

I know this child, that window,
so like my own growing up.
From my bedroom I could see
into the neighbor's apartment,
the Greek lady who kept cats.
I was allowed to visit the cats on Sundays.

I know that telephone
which I was not allowed to touch.
It brought news to Mama
from Daddy who was off winning the war.
or Uncle Irv or Uncle Jerry, or cousin Bill,
also doing their parts.

I know those bears, the big one especially,
though I preferred dolls with long hair
wearing the kinds of dresses I wanted,
in soft blues or bright yellows,
and straw hats with ribbons.
I would have had a closetful.

I know that boy, the one whose parents
brought him over, through the war
each carrying one straw bag
crammed with everything they needed.
And all he brought, he told me in second grade,
was one Big Bear, one Little Bear.

He carried the rest of it in his *kopf*,
he said, pointing to his head,
his eyes wide and deep as pools.
"Speak American," I hissed at him.
When he burst into tears, I was surprised.
"I thought I was," he whispered back.

4. ONLY A PHOTOGRAPH

It is only a photograph, Daddy,
and you weeping like a boy
whose feelings have been hurt.
Like a girl with a skinned knee.
I could call the doctor on the phone
if you would let me dial it.
Here, hold Little Bear,
he keeps away the brown shirts,
the ones who took away your Mama,
your baby brother, with the wide eyes,
deep like the pools you swam in
when you were off with Uncle Sid.

But you have me, now. And Mommy.
And the new baby coming.
We are your family instead.
Enough is enough, Mama says.
Why are you crying, Daddy?
Is it the photograph again,
the boy with the two bears
who never made it out of the house?
Who died in the bombings or the camps
or the fire, or the ovens, those changing stories,
when no one came, as you always come,
to find me and take me home again.

KRISTALLNACHT IN HAMBURG

We turn into the street
where glass had once been broken
in every synagogue,
in every Jewish store,
the street shards shining up
at the street lights,
those lights shining down
like uncaring stars.

Tonight, everything is quiet.
Somewhere off to the right
a band is playing in a bar,
jazz, maybe, something light.
Not all Germans remember
this is the night.
It is eighty years later,
their great grandparents' sin,
only a story, a history,
they will have one of their own.

But still, we are all broken.
But still, we are all glass.

ALPHABET OF EVIL

What is the alphabet of evil?
Auschwitz,
Buchenwald,
Chelmno,
the names of camps
rolling off the tongue,
the tongue lolling in the mouth,
the mouth hanging open,
broken teeth,
a gasp of breath,
the alphabet of death.

What is the alphabet of evil?
Dachau,
Esterwegen,
Flossenberg,
Gurs,
the names of camps
cramping the stomach,
the stomach drained of blood,
blood staining the ground,
a last breath,
the alphabet of death.

What is the alphabet of evil?
It begins with Adolph Hitler,
goes to the Sonderkommandos,
ends with the ordinary citizen
turning in his neighbor,
a shekel for a traitor,
a groat for a Jew.

What is the alphabet of evil?
Small letters
we all know how to say,
and hope we are never asked
in our ordinary lives
to say them.

BLUE THE COLOR OF HOPE: ON THE SHIP ST. LOUIS

Blue road the color of hope,
Waves like tzitzit on a prayer shawl,
Sea lanes our only map.

Sea lanes our only map,
We speak the Sh'ma into the air.
It whispers back promises.

It whispers back promises
Sweet as the honey
On the alef bet slate.

On the alef bet slate
We licked the honey off,
Our first hunger for knowledge.

Our first hunger for knowledge
Did not lead us to understand
The depth of hate.

The depth of hate
Pushed us onto this boat
Where blue is the color of hope.

RETURN TO THE REICH: ON THE SHIP ST. LOUIS

Even Cuba did not want us,
Denying immigrant papers,
Sending us back on the blue road.

Sending us back on the blue road,
This time to Florida where lights
Of Miami sent Morse signals.

Miami sent Morse signals
Denying us entrance,
Waving us back towards Germany.

Waving us back towards Germany
Where all the windows
And lights of Kristallnacht were broken,

The lights of Kristallnacht were broken
Shattered like our lives,
Strong warnings of what was to come.

Strong warnings of what was to come
Had sent us into exile, our homes behind us,
And the horror of the ovens ahead.

The horror of the ovens ahead
Yet to be revealed,
We chanced the blue road again.

We chanced the blue road again,
Waves like bony fingers of ghosts.
Drowning would have been a softer death.

Drowning would have been a softer death.
But even then, prayers did not suffice,
For we were sent back home.

We were sent back home
To a place where murderers waited.
Even Cuba did not want us.

Author's note: A few people with proper papers were let off in Cuba,
but Miami and the rest of America sent the Jewish refugees back
to Germany. Some were allowed into Great Britain, Belgium,
France and the Netherlands. Half of the passengers survived the
war, the rest did not. All would have survived had they been let
into Cuba or the USA.

EVEN DACHAU IS ONLY A PLACE

"Even Dachau is only a place. . ."
—Judith B. Kerman,
Uses of the Fantastic in Literature of the Holocaust

Such an ordinary town for murders.
Such a secondary train station.
Even with the barbed wires,
who could imagine the horrors,
except when the doors opened,
when the smoke belched,
when the guards scratching their balls
with a left hand, and laughing,
tightened the fingers of their right hands
on the triggers of their guns.

Such an ordinary place,
and that little man Hitler,
with his silly mustache
and raised arm salute,
such an ordinary man.

MAJDANEK: WINTER 1941-1942

This was the lethal winter
when men were shot for being cold,
for being slow, for sneezing, for freezing,
the edge of the camp grounds a spoiled land
littered with dead bodies. When prisoners fell,
the bullets inside them were like ice pellets.
That killing, while pleasant to the guards,
was much too slow and labored.
The next year they had no such fun.
The Black Path lead to the ovens,
where Death played chess
on the breastbones of the Jews.
Do not tell me no one smelled that evil
as it rose into the air like smoke.
The people who lived close by
could tell pirogi from cabbage.
They knew when the neighbors grilled kielbasa,
whether it was pork, beef, veal, lamb.
Surely, they could smell
the burning of human flesh,
that crisp sharpness.
Nothing like it I am told.
Perhaps they did not care because
it was sweet smelling,
and so very final.

"ICH BIN A YOOD"

> After reading a Holocaust anecdote in Barbara Rush's
> *Book of Jewish Women's Tales*

The rabbi's daughter,
savaged by a thousand cuts,
a thousand bites
from Grayze's dogs,
called out—for each cut, each bite—
that she was a Jew and would not kneel.
She died, on her knees,
but not kneeling
for she stood upright at the throne of G-d.
G-d, I wish I had such courage
to not-kneel in the face
of outrage, the teeth of tyranny,
the knives of the unholy.
Instead, I change the channels,
I turn the page,
I write a small poem
in the rabbi's daughter's honor,
I, who do not even know her name.

PHOTOGRAPH OF A DEAD CHILD
ON A GHETTO STREET

Such an ordinary sight, three people walk by,
hardly giving her a glance,
as if she were a rabbit dead in a field,
or an old dog who died by the fire.
Just another piece of drek on the cobbles
to be taken away by the garbage collector.
Three hundred calories a day, such rations
could not sustain a growing child,
so she has stopped growing.
Her feet, her legs, her face stiff and cold,
like pavement and as gray.
This child who once danced
about her mother's kitchen,
a bit of afikomin in her hand,
the four questions so lately in her mouth.
Dance, little Hannahleh, Chaya, Gittel, Rachael,
whatever your name was when you were alive.
Dance on the streets of Heaven,
for you shall never dance here again.

IN THE LODZ GHETTO AT DINNER

The man has been erased, but his outline
still eats with us every evening,
still leaves an imprint of his body
on the bed next to his grieving wife.

He who had made so little impression
living, now lives large though disappeared,
as if he takes all the sustenance
from our meager portions.

If only we could learn from his dying
how to live, suck protein from the air,
distribute it to the hungry, make life
out of his all but forgotten death.

ACORNS

First birches, like marble statues,
guard the small sleepers.
Then oak bends down to take them,
swollen with night, into her arms.

Hide me, they cry, before the guns.
Hide me, they cry, before the bullets.
Hide me, they cry, before the hate
turns them to timber, to bone, to ash.

There are not enough trees left
in all the forest to save them,
these babes in the woods,
these tiny nestlings, these little acorns.

SEWER RAT

Hiding in the sewer,
this little rat,
rattus rattus,
no whiskers, tail,
only a grubby gray face,
runnels of tears
a lighter shade of gray.
Yes, I know it is a child,
a Yiddishe pisher,
gender yet to be determined.
Yet, who can tell in all that filth?
Here with the other vermin,
squeaking instead of speaking.
Call it enforced mutism,
camouflaged, hidden in drek,
about what you'd expect,
where disguise is the only answer
to death.

OVENS

"...when cinders smart the eyes and we begin
to spit soot."
—Simon Schama

The old witch's ovens never stop smoking,
that delectable house reeks of roast pork,
not a kosher smell, but tempting.
Along the property lines, a minyan of bones
dances the hora whenever another piece of meat
comes into sight, a warning never heeded.
There's only one word for what she does to them.
Speak it and you become a collaborator.
Just a shudder will do, and a curse,
even as your eyes turn red,
even as sooty spit pools
along with the candy
in your slackening mouth.

MENGELE

There is no wisdom, just cunning:
wolf's quiet padding on the trail,
snake curled fernlike
at the turning of the road,
spider hidden in the web's shimmer.

There is no conscience, just patterns,
camouflage, the watcher in the hide,
sharp teeth at the throat,
venom in the ankle's bend,
sticky filaments sewn into a shroud.

There is no atonement, just silence
in the belly of the wolf,
a narrow parting of the grass,
spider's larder silently shutting,
when death has done

its deed.

TWIN EXPERIMENT

The necessary: a matching pair of children,
surgical table, handcuffs, a sharp knife.
Nothing more. One twin expired of fear,
too quick for the doctor, the other cowering.

On the floor, he tries to make a barrier of a chair.
It was laughable, really, so the guards laughed.
One spat at the child and the doctor scolded.
Not for the laugh, but for sputum in the surgery.

The live child's skin was no fortress, held back nothing.
The knife entered silent as a thief, stole him away.
The ribs showed like the arch of cathedral stone.
The doctor worshipped there, without mercy or prayer.

Both bodies went into the cart. The Shoah ate them whole.
If God is watching, He is weeping. May He choke on every soul.

FOR A CHILD DYING OF TYPHOID IN A LABOR CAMP

She wore her modest typhoid
like a gown.

    It graced her, kept her warm
    even as she grew cold.
Red blossoms on her cheeks,
but soon they will fall.
She will never be old,

    never grow into cynicism,
stale in her beliefs.

    It is a relief to know
she will not suffer time,
will not, in her delirium,
think of food or water anymore.

    Death is not a smokestack here,
but an opening door.

WHAT THE OVEN IS NOT

The oven is no sanctuary.
The food knows it, the Jew knows it.
Oil poured on, water bubbles out.
We crisp as easily as chicken,
though not as kosher.
Cancers, like stuffing, fill the gaps.
I do not know, nor do I care
what you think of the Shoah.
I have spent half a lifetime
writing about it, intruding into the pain.
My family—ever early adopters—
escaped via immigration and long luck.
There is a sickness here,
but it bears no name.
The oven knows it, and does not say.

HOLOCAUST STORIES

These are the stories
no one wants to tell,
but must be told.
Memory cannot hold them fast,
They fade with the death
of the last survivor.
Victim, guard, even they
do not remember it all.

But story binds the actual
to the true.
It is no coincidence
that history ends this way.
We make it true again, truer,
because story sticks
when memory fails.

Water over stone, day by day,
leaves but a small impression.
Centuries later,
with searching fingers
we read the truth
of the rounded rocks.
What was lost
is found again
in that reading.

UN-SEEING

How to un-see the photograph:
three men, one playing accordion,
eight smiling women in uniforms,
taking a brief break.
They pose, grin, hide the cigs,
(it was the forties, you know)
trade anecdotes about work:
who dropped dead in fright,
how many they lost to starvation.
The fourth ofen had a Fehlfunktion.
That photograph title?
"Laughing at Auschwitz,"
while Anne Frank wastes away there
dreaming of writing
if only she had some paper,
if only she had a pen,
if only she had some time.

AFTER EFFECT

DIALOGUE

"To write poetry after Auschwitz is barbaric."
—Theodor Adorno, German sociologist and philosopher

". . .at home a task/Awaits me: To create poetry after Auschwitz."
—Tadeusz Rozewicz, from *I Did Espy a Marvelous Monster*

1.

How can we talk to one another about history
when we cannot talk about art?
Even the martyrs sang hymns
on their way to the fire,
and Jesus spoke verse
while hanging on his pole.
Can we not make poems
about the six million?
Do we need a German, even a half Jew,
to tell us that?

2.

Do you deny us the children's drawings
of butterflies at Theresienstadt.
or the melodies Beethoven made
in the labor camp of his deafness?
We are brought to grace
through the poetry of suffering:
uplifted, gifted, strengthened,
given breadth and breath.

3.

The stick across the palm,
the buttocks, that able teacher
we swear never to emulate,
though history reminds us
the impulse is never far from our hands.
We conflate the strike
against the soles of the feet
with the souls we defeat.

4.

Let us protest, praise,
let passions' fires,
let poetry align us
with our deeper desires.
Mene, mene, tekel, upharsin,
we are counted and weighed.
Only in poetry
is that final price paid.

5.

This is not an argument,
it is a dialogue,
the world begun again
with a word.

ELIE WIESEL IS DEAD (AFTER E.E.CUMMINGS)

Elie Wiesel is dead
who parsed night
fought the darkness
with a yahrzeit candle,
made reluctant witnesses
of us all. So how do you like
that eighty-seven-year survivor,
Herr Hitler, while you
have been rotten and rotting
in your dirty underwear
all these long years later.

WHEN WE WERE PUT IN CAMPS

My first camp was spare,
double bunk beds, thin mattresses,
the call of a loon from the lake.
I got up at four to muck out stalls.
My boyfriend kissed me
after the square dance.
This is not about that camp,
where lanyards were an option,
and swimming was not.
This is about the litany of horrors—
Dachau, Sobibor, Auschwitz,
a roll call of infamy.
This is about the dark swallows
like avenging angels
circling the smokestacks.
About thin potato gruel in cracked cups.
About bald skeletons in filthy rags
digging their own mass graves.
Do not be fooled again.
Their people are our people.
The lamp lifts for all of us.
Hijabs that cover the hair
also cover the need of aching hearts.
If you build camps again,
one day they will come for you,
they will come for us.
And I will not be there
with my small poem as warning,
for it will already have been burned.

YELLOW STAR: A SONG WITHOUT MUSIC

We sit at home and watch the news,
Our conscience caught upon the screen:
Black against white, Muslims, Jews.
We push the mute to damp the scene.

We send a check off for the cause
And feel a savior, right and clean.
And then, without a moment's pause,
We change the channel on the screen.

> Too late my friends for turning back,
> I am what I am, you are what you are,
> Overhead the sky goes black.
> We all must wear the yellow star.

We hear the sound of breaking glass,
Ground under boot heel, very fine.
Life is taken though it should pass,
And you have grabbed up what was mine.

Once again the wind is sighing,
Once again the words come hard,
Once again the young are dying
Under the eyes of a sullen guard.

> Too late my friends for turning back,
> I am what I am, you are what you are.
> Overhead the sky goes black.
> We all must wear the yellow star.

We are what we are, the ape made man.
We wield the stick as tool, as gun.
We do what we do and not what we can
And heaven help us if we run.

The signs have come, and they have gone,
Like gods they suddenly appear.
The signs are burning on the lawn
And I am old enough to care.

Too late my friends for turning back.
I am what I am, you are what you are,
Overhead the sky goes black.
We all must wear the yellow star.

SILVER SHIRTS

Here come the silver shirts again,
American-born Nazis,
willing to enslave
their black neighbors,
send the Jews on a new diaspora.

Once arm in arm with the Bund,
marching under a banner
of an embarrassed-looking
George Washington,
they tried to take our government.

Their children in summer camps
dedicated to Hitler,
they skated along the fringe
of an increasingly diverse
America.

Sound familiar? It should.
Take a deep breath.
What you smell is human roast
in an oven, rotting black flesh
hanging from a tree.

It is an old fight,
but a necessary one.
Be the patriot, not the traitor
intent on closing you down
to the size of his own small heart.

RETURN

The Cossacks Are Back. May the Hills Tremble
—*New York Times* headline, March 2013

O, my people, memories are short,
but bones remember. And like the hills,
we tremble.

Cossacks were the reason we left our homes,
neighbors, graves of our grandparents,
braving the ocean.

They were why we left the old lives,
so our girls could work as milliners,
eyes weeping black tears.

Why our sons could drag carts behind them,
like cattle, sweating patches dark as blood
under their arms.

O, my people, revenge has a long lash.
The skin remembers. But unlike the hills,
we do not remain.

TZIMMES

The Cossack wind blows
across the craven Rockies,
fanning the flames.
Taras Bulba be damned;
these are not the people
I want in my kitchen,
shooting off their guns and mouths
glancing at my oven meaningfully,
where the tzimmes simmers.
They eat Jews like me,
the ones with small pearls in our ears,
bookcases full of heavy fiction.
It's time to move again,
before another Shoah
shows up at the door.

DARKNESS DESCENDENT

I read the news carelessly at first,
scanning for what is true, not true,
as if that makes a difference anymore.
My eye rests on an article: 75.

The number itself begins that tumble.
not dollars, not stock market,
but people, demonstrators,
as I have been in my time.
Those caught up in a protest five years ago,
about to be executed in Egypt.

I think of the Jews, the diaspora,
the exodus, crossing the water.
How we exalted to Miriam's tambourine
when Egyptians—not just 75—
but by the thousands—
drowned in the hungry sea.

Surely, we know better now,
not to exalt for death.
Yet how many protesting
are sent back daily into darkness?
Over 700 more rotting in Egyptian jails
waiting for the axe to fall.

Once again, we are cavemen howling
at the moon's eclipse,
washing our hands at crucifixions,
moaning in Hollywood horror

as darkness descends.

SHOES: HOLOCAUST MUSEUM, WASHINGTON D.C.

I walk with foreknowledge into the museum,
sure it has nothing to teach me.
I've read the biographies, watched the movies,
sat through *Shoah* three times, *Schindler's List*.
I've touched a weeping stone in Heidelberg
for a synagogue set alight by hate;
interviewed Survivors; dated a Survivor's child;
did the research; listened to a friend retell his childhood
in a Polish labor camp, forced to dive into the midden,
whenever the commandant's car drove by.

So why now, standing by a pyramid of shoes,
from a liberated camp,
am I stunned, undone, incapable of moving on?
Is it the sheer number of shoes in the pile,
or the one on the top exactly the size
of my granddaughter's foot?

MESSENGER

"Man is the messenger who forgets
the message."
—Rabbi Joshua Herschel

He reaches into his bag,
hand searching for the message,
but it must have blown away
during his long ride.

Once he might have memorized,
memorialized the message,
the sense of it softened
by mnemonics and a song.

Once he might have closed his eyes,
read the message as if written
on the backs of his eyelids,
graven in ink on his palm.

Now he makes it up,
using the sonorous tones
of a storyteller, newsman,
politician, consummate liar.

No one cares.

SLOUCHING TOWARDS BETHLEHEM

"Israel Convicts a Palestinian Poet:
   for a poem they say incites violence and supports terror."
—Unknown Headline

Yeats is crouched in his grave,
preparing to turn over like meat on a spit.
One more round and he is done.

Jerusalem, where King David wrote poems
about politics and self-doubt has been cancelled.
The Garden is closed for the millennium.

Lions no longer lie down with lambs,
for all the psalmists are in prisons
on one side of the Golan Heights or another.

I am waiting for the summons on my door,
that invitation to prison, that long slouch
to the old city, Bethlehem or D.C.

TALKING AUSCHWITZ

"Poland has imposed limits on speech about
the Holocaust."
—NPR

If the Poles can no longer speak
then I shall speak.
Every poem will be about
the ovens.

If the Poles can no longer talk
then I shall talk.
Every period, every comma,
a memory.

If the Poles can no longer guide,
then I shall guide.
Take my hand, together
we will walk through fire to be free.

OPEN LETTER TO JOHN GALLIANO

> "Excuse me John, but as an expert, who do you think
>   would look more fashionable entering the gas chamber,
>   you in your pink triangle or me with my yellow Star of David?"
> —Dr. Marcel Sislowitz

Your beloved Hitler would see no difference
between my yellow star, your pink triangle,
except in the names of our camps,
except in the countryside where they blot the landscape.
We would both be made to dance with Death,
our designer clothing striped pajamas,
our only jewels the gold in our teeth.
You would call out for your mother,
I would pray to my old Jehovah,
but neither could answer us in the showers,
the walls too thick, the gas too quick,
the world too careless of its treasures.
Afterwards, your friend, the little man,
failed painter, would tap a victory dance
on our scorched bones. This is the truth of it.
Unlike you, I have no reason to lie.

THE RIVERS OF BABYLON: IN MEMORIAM

I am told there is grass at Auschwitz,
and people picnic there again
beside the iron maw that swallowed
the expendable children. Good wine,
white from the Rhineland, flows
from open necks, down laughing mouths.
And papers litter the ominous mounds,
receptacles that cry for truth.

If we forget these, will our tongues
cleave to dry mouths, or hands
hang helpless at our sides?
Unstrung, the harps of this new exile
whisper from the swaying trees:
This exile soft, this new G-d quick
to ease our memories.

It is with humanity more fine we choose
to hymn the dead alive with laughter,
then wail the grave, and martyred Jews?

THE WIDOW MANDELSTAM

See her, that old lady,
muttering into the wind.
She has not lost her mind,
but found it here,
here in the cold Soviet camp
where Jews kindle together
hoping for warmth.
Here where even birds,
starvelings of the sky,
fall stiffly to the ground.
But her mouth holds
her husband's ashes.
She recreates him
syllable by syllable,
poem by poem.
There is no love greater.
Or more terrifying.

ON VIEWING A PHOTOGRAPH OF DONALD
AT THE WESTERN WALL

Perched on his head,
a black knish of silence,
the yarmulke looks ready to flee.

His hand demands payment
from the wall, a wail
that confuses wish with deed.

Face, misappropriating prayer,
mirrors his greed, his need
for approval; still a schoolboy

with a father who never gave love
only money which to this day
he mistakes for passion.

The wall crumbles beneath his hand,
history defeated by anger,
confused by the stutter of his mind.

This is midrash. Even the orthodox
know him for a pretender,
an offender of the faith,

no friend of Israel but the harbinger
of chaos, bringer of ploughshares
he intends to beat back into swords.

MITZVAHS

AND MIRACLES

LULEK AND THE RABBI: APRIL 11, 1945

He was seven, yet older
than the rabbi who rescued him,
plucking him from the rubble of history.

He could not laugh or cry or play like a child,
had to be taught truth, honor
above that last cold potato snatched
from the plate of a dying man.

He learned trust slowly, love later, G-d last
who had left him in that place,
cold despite the fires,
alive despite death.

Does he, a rabbi himself, now dream
of green fields, flocks of sheep,
a rustic Germany, or does he see only
swallows flying over smokestacks
singing Kaddish to the uncaring sky?

THE TROCHENBROD MIRACLE

"The little girl wasn't more than 3 years old. . . very very sick,
and she died. . .we left the little girl under a pile of leaves,
and we figured . . .we'll go and bury her. When we came back
to bury her, she was breathing! Just barely."
—Avro Bendavid-Val, from *The Heavens Are Empty,*
Discovering the Lost Town of Trochenbrod

The trees hid the miracle, bless them.
Their heavy trunks, limbs twisted
as an old man's fingers, made a wall.

The bunker nursed the miracle, bless it.
Dug deep into the earth, it made a nest,
a sanctuary, a hospice, a home.

The leaves blanketed the miracle, bless them.
They hid her small body, not dead,
not quite dead yet, till she was ready.

The town mothers fed the miracle, bless them.
They opened beaks like frantic birds,
dripping water into her mouth.

The town fathers held her close, bless them.
They gave her their own warmth,
pulled from the burning of their hearts.

The world gave her back life, bless it,
so she could bless G-d with her living,
her goodness, after the war.

NO ESCAPE

"In this story you don't escape the words."
—Simon Schama

We Jews never escape the word,
the alef-bet made sweeter
by honey in the mouth
of each new reader.
We tongue the letters
till they flow like mother's milk.

I remember my first books:
stories about kings and fairies,
a bunch of ducklings
crossing a Boston street,
cats by the millions,
and a bull that refused to fight.

Nothing sweeter than that,
a beeline to the brain,
and years of pilpul after.

IF ONE CHILD IS SAVED

If one child is saved,
we call it a miracle.
If many children die,
a Holocaust.
We have no word
for the in-between,
only for those
moments of peace
with a small p.
Perhaps if we did,
We would have
a record crop
of ploughshares.
We could spend our days
listening to small hands
playing clapping games,
not hiding in closets
or cellars, or holes.
If one child and one child
are saved.
And one more
and one more.
If we could find
the capital P
hidden away in the duck's egg,
along with Kostchai's heart,
perhaps.
Perhaps.
It is an old story.
The oldest.
It is a good dream.
The best.

THIS IS THE MIRACLE

Not the escape from the whip,
the bullet, the chimney.
Not safety across three waters.
Not the poem kept in memory's palace.
Not a warm house, cold cider,
hot bath every night.
Not even you in my bed,
who never had to flee anything.
Think of it: my grandchild's hand in mine,
as she sleeps without fear,
knowing nightmares always become day.

That is the true miracle.
The only one.

I WITNESS

"The human soul does not want to be
advised or fixed or saved. It simply wants
to be witnessed...."
—Parker Palmer

I hear you.
I see you.
I witness.

I hear what you said.
I see what you saw.
I witness.

I feel what you felt.
I kneel where you knelt.
I rise where you have risen.

I see your moment of grace,
Your incandescent space,
Your smokestack of despair.

I am your yahrzeit candle,
Your left-life hook,
Your open-closed book.

And I witness.

KADDISH

It is all here, you know,
the darkness, the light,
though sometimes difficult
to know which is which.
My people escaped the Tsar's Fists,
to find ourselves free
of the Shoah as well.
But no Jew truly escapes
that time, those places,
unscarred, unscathed.
I have no numbers on my arms,
But I have studied the charts,
the cities, the deaths,
till I know them by heart.
Knowing means remembrance.
We Jews may be short
much of the time.
But our memories,
our memories are long.

ACKNOWLEDGEMENTS

"First Woman, Lilith," © 2017, *Before the Vote, After,* Leveller's Press.

"Rusulka," © 2001, Mythic Delirium Magazine.

"That Old Anti-Semite, Jakob Grimm," © 2019,
Other Covenants Anthology.

"The Child, The Bears, The War: Four Views," © 2020, *Contemporary Writers Confronting the Holocaust,* New Voices Project ™.

"Alphabet of Evil," © 2008, published in *America at Work,* edited by Lee Bennett Hopkins, Margaret K. McElderry Books, New York.

"Blue the Color of Hope: On the Ship St. Louis, Return to the Reich: On the Ship St. Louis," both from anthology © 2017, *Traveling the Blue Road: Poems of the Sea,* edited by Lee Bennett Hopkins, Quarto Books.

"God's Carton" and "Light" from *The Last Robot,* © 2021, *Shoreline of Infinity,* Edinburgh, Scotland.

"Majdanek: Winter 1941-1942," © 2019, Coffin Bell Journal.

"Photograph of a Dead Child on a Ghetto Street," © 2012, *Conclave Literary Magazine,* Issue 4.

"In the Lodz Ghetto at Dinner," First verse © 2018, from *Mapping the Bones,* Philomel Books.

"Acorns," © 2018, *Mapping the Bones,* Philomel Books.

ABOUT THE AUTHOR

JANE YOLEN, called the "Hans Christian Andersen of America" because of her work with fairy tales, is also a fine poet. *Kaddish* is her 13th book of poems for adult readers.

In March, 2021 her 400th book was published. She works across all genres—children's books and adult books: science fiction, fantasy, historical novels, storybooks, short stories, cookbooks, music books, nonfiction, anthologies, collections—even a novel in verse. She has written musicals, and the lyrics for many bands.

She writes a poem a day which she sends to over a thousand subscribers. Six colleges and universities have given her honorary doctorates for her body of work. Her latest awards have been from the Jewish Book Council, the World Fantasy Association, a Massachusetts State Book Award, and a nomination by the USA for the International Astrid Lindgren Award. She lives in New England and in Scotland.

For more information, visit *www.janeyolen.com*